Abnormal Brain Sonnets

Also by David W. McFadden

Animal Spirits
Anonymity Suite
The Art of Darkness
Be Calm, Honey
Canadian Sunset
Country of the Open Heart
Five Star Planet
The Great Canadian Sonnet
Great Lakes Suite
Gypsy Guitar
I Don't Know
An Innocent in Cuba
An Innocent in Ireland
An Innocent in Newfoundland
An Innocent in Scotland
Intense Pleasure
A Knight in Dried Plums
Letters from the Earth to the Earth
A Little Kindness
Mother Died Last Summer
My Body Was Eaten by Dogs: Selected Poems of David McFadden
A New Romance
On the Road Again
The Ova Yogas
A Pair of Baby Lambs
The Poem Poem
Poems Worth Knowing
The Poet's Progress
The Saladmaker
Shouting Your Name Down the Well: Tankas and Haiku
The Sun Will Not Shine Forever
There'll Be Another
Three Stories and Ten Poems
What's the Score?
Why Are You So Long and Sweet? Collected Long Poems of David W. McFadden
Why Are You So Sad? Selected Poems of David W. McFadden

Abnormal Brain Sonnets

David W. McFadden

Mansfield Press

a stuart ross book

Printed in Canada

Library and Archives Canada Cataloguing in Publication

McFadden, David, 1940-, author
Abnormal brain sonnets / David W. McFadden.

Poems.
ISBN 978-1-77126-097-8 (paperback)

I. Title.

PS8525.F32A64 2015 C811'.54 C2015-906202-0

Editor for the press: Stuart Ross
Typesetting: Stuart Ross
Cover design: Denis De Klerck
Author photo: Stuart Ross

The publication of *Abnormal Brain Sonnets* has been generously supported by the Canada Council for the Arts and the Ontario Arts Council.

ONTARIO ARTS COUNCIL
CONSEIL DES ARTS DE L'ONTARIO
an Ontario government agency
un organisme du gouvernement de l'Ontario

Canada Council for the Arts Conseil des arts du Canada

Mansfield Press Inc.
25 Mansfield Avenue, Toronto, Ontario, Canada M6J 2A9
Publisher: Denis De Klerck
www.mansfieldpress.net

For Carmela, Allison, David
and all the others
who help and heal

Contents

1

1. Dave Gets Born

Before I was born I wasn't a baby—
Just something floating in the skies—
But then I came out from my mother
And also came out a pair of eyes.
I was lying in a little lake of love
And away off in the distance I saw
An entire city of houses far below.
Farther out was a lachrymose lagoon.

My mother was holding me in her arms
And she showed me all the little houses.
I seemed to be way up on a mountain
But it was just the Niagara Escarpment.
And then I realized I was going somewhere—
Something was happening, I didn't know what.

2. Dave Dies and Is Reborn

My mother found me in my crib dead-cold.
She screamed and threw a blanket over me
And ran with me to the doctor's office.
The doctor said there was nothing he could do
For there was no breathing in or out.
I was cold as ice and that wasn't nice.
But then my mother cleverly pinched my toes—
And I started breathing through my nose.

From then on every day my mother would say
That I was very close to death that day.
She was so happy that I didn't die
I almost got tired of hearing her sigh.
I liked my mother but I didn't like her
When she kept forgetting to change my diaper.

3. Images on the Wall

In my crib things were often damp
And my room was very small indeed.
There were no pictures on the walls,
Nor were there any on the ceiling.
I was too small to look out the window.
Some beautiful images appeared on the wall.
It was like a painting but they were moving.
I think there were a tiger and some angels.

In my small room I breathed in and out.
I seemed to think I was going to grow up
But nobody told me how that could be done.
Now and then my mother checked to see me.
I think she liked me but I don't remember.
The images on the wall were what I liked.

4. Hunky-Dory

Once I started to take my first steps
My parents seemed to become very happy.
I took a step and then I took another
And soon I made an actual word.
I said hunky-dory. I didn't know
What it meant but it was something that
My parents were always saying at the time.
They said hunky-dory, so I said it too.

I liked saying it, so I kept saying it,
And Mummy and Daddy laughed when I did.
Then I realized hunky was another word
For hanky. Dory was a word for the door,
So I took a few steps towards the door
And then I put the hanky on the knob.

5. Balmoral Avenue

We lived at 175 Balmoral Avenue
In Hamilton, Ontario, Canada.
My father worked at the Steel Company.
My mother worked at the Firestone Plant.
May took care of me and I loved her.
I loved her when she put me on her knee
And showed me how to flip through magazines
Even though I didn't know how to read.

She taught me how to understand numbers.
There would be a number on the top of the page
But once in a while there wouldn't be a number
And I said to May that wasn't fair.
She said it was at the bottom of the page—
We agreed that wasn't nice for little kids.

6. May Morrell's Magazines

I enjoyed it when May Morrell put me
To bed one lazy afternoon.
I was only three. I asked her if
She would get into bed with me
And she thought that was a nice idea.
I was so happy I forgot about nasty
Page numbers that confused children.
Okay for grown-ups but not for kids.

Meanwhile Mother was still at Firestone.
She was doing her bit for the war effort.
She was making, with others, parachutes.
She liked her job but she didn't care
For women who were visibly pregnant
One day, but the next day they weren't.

7. Sniff the Flowers

One day I slip out of the door
And find myself in another world
And where the heck is May Morrell?
And I don't know where my parents are.
I stroll through the grass and enjoy
Tall flowers I've never seen before.
I walk up to a decrepit garage.
I sniff the flowers and something else.

I know that if I turn around I'll see
The back of the house, but I don't
Want to see it. I want to imagine it.
But very slowly I turn around and I
See how my house looks from the back
And I sense that I am growing up.

8. My First Hockey Stick

I was four years old or maybe three
But my mother didn't mind if I strolled
Along the street alone. Not much traffic.
I didn't go far. Some little girls were
Playing with chalk on the blackboard.
I blustered in and told them I could read.
They didn't want to know. They said go home.
Seems they didn't like boys who could read.

I was sad. It really hurt a lot.
It was the first time my heart was broken.
Mother bought me a little hockey stick
And I shot that puck all the way up
The stairs. It made an awful racket.
My mother wouldn't let me play anymore.

9. Cannon to Roxborough

Mother didn't care if I played on the porch
But she didn't like me playing in the alley.
One day she chased me and I ran
All the way from Cannon to Roxborough.
Mother was running behind me, so
I put on a big shot of juice,
But Mother put on a bigger shot.
"I'll catch him," said a bigger kid.

Mother said she'd prefer to catch me
Without another kid getting involved
Even if that kid was a rotten stinker.
She finally got a hold of my shirt
And then she pulled me down and sat on me.
She said don't ever do a thing like that.

10. Grandma's House

The older kids were very nice to me.
They let me sit on somebody's wagon.
As they pulled the wagon along I noticed
The wagon had slats that separated.
I'd look down as the sidewalk went by
And I could see the pavement going along.
In the air I noticed a plane going by.
And a smaller plane was being towed along.

The older kids said the plane was going
To drop a bomb on my grandma's house.
I believed them and I started to cry.
Pretty soon they said they were sorry.
They took me up to their porch and I looked
At the Niagara Escarpment up above.

P.S.—The smaller "plane" that was being towed was actually spraying chemicals to kill insects (I think, but what would I know at such a young age—this around 1943). Spraying chemicals like that is seldom done today. Also, strangely enough, the airplane, and the smaller plane being towed, were actually heading directly towards my grandmother's house.

11. The Avalon

Gordon pulled my wagon up and down
And I'd look through the slats as the
Sidewalk went by. It was fun.
I was four, and he was much older.
I guess he was about seven or eight.
I envied his high leather boots.
Gordon and Sammy asked my mother if
They could take me to the Avalon.

The Avalon was on Ottawa Street.
We were sitting on the left side.
At first I couldn't understand
What was happening, it seemed a dream.
But I didn't believe Gordon when he said
The real people were behind the screen.

12. Kindergarten Time

It was time for me to go to school.
I really didn't know what school was.
For some reason I never understood
I started kindergarten in October.
The other kids started in September.
I loved to watch the colourful leaves.
Mother held my hand along the street
Then left me to the fate I deserved.

I think Mother was glad I was gone.
And come to think of it I was also.
I can't remember anything at all
From October until next April
When we moved to Barons Avenue
And I started to remember everything.

13. Canadian Artillery Guns

My first school was Memorial.
I don't remember very much about it.
I'm trying to remember but my brain
Doesn't recall anything at all.
I can't remember kids short or tall.
The name of the teacher I can't remember.
All my thoughts have only drawn a blank.
What happened from October to November?

I remember a teacher. I can't recall
If she was nice or not. She was short.
And there was a man who was tall.
We were allowed to go for lunch. They
Let us climb all over our First
World War Canadian artillery gun.

14. Featherstone Point

My second school was W. H. Ballard.
We sat on the floor every day,
Except for Miss Robinson who was tall,
So tall we couldn't see the top of her head.
I was the only kid who knew the alphabet.
There was Kenny Kernaghan, Brian Brock,
And others I can't recall sorry to say.
I think a lot of them have gone to heaven.

They were too young to go to hell.
And when summer arrived Mom and Dad
Took me and my baby brother to the lake.
We went to the shore of Lake Ontario—
And my dad built a cabin on the sands
Of Lake Erie: Featherstone Point.

15. My Dick

Miss McFarlane was my Grade 1 teacher.
There were forty-one kids in the class.
I was the only kid who could read.
Everyone even Miss McFarlane
Thought I was a genius (but I wasn't).
I could read—May Morrell had taught me to.
I felt jealous when Miss McFarlane
Spent an hour talking to a male friend.

In Grade 2 we also had Miss McFarlane.
But her boy friend didn't show up this time.
I was sitting in the front of the class
And all of a sudden Miss McFarlane's
Face went all red. She looked at me.
My fly was open, my dick was sticking out.

16. The Korean War

Also in Grade 2 Miss McFarlane
Insisted I stand at the front of the room.
She produced a page for me to read,
To show the other kids I had a brain.
I had to stand there and recite a story,
But when it came to the word "ocean"
I could spell it but I couldn't read it.
The ocean was so vast I couldn't cross it.

In Grade 3 we hated Miss Pollox.
Except the principal, Mr. Force,
Who was always pestering and trying
To get her to have sex with him, I think.
It was all about the Korean War
And soon we would have to go and die.

17. Dead Was All He Answered

Half of the kids in the class stayed
In Grade 4 but the others went
Into Grade 5. The teacher was
Mr. Warren, and boy was he ever cool.
He sat cross-legged on his desk and
Laughed about the squirrels in his yard.
He told us about Silas coming back
To help him build the load and pitching it.

I wish I could remember more about
Mr. Warren. I'll see if that small
Sailing cloud will hit or miss the moon.
It hit the moon. Then there were three,
The moon, the little silver cloud, and she.
Warren, she asked. Dead, was all he answered.

18. Torn T-Shirts

In school things weren't all that interesting.
I remember Miss Addleton who was old.
My mother and some of my uncles and aunts
Were in her class several decades before.
The boys wanted to get more ice time
But the only time we could get was five a.m.
That didn't bother me in the slightest.
I didn't want to be no hockey star.

I just wanted to be a little poet.
Tommy Shay was my best friend that year.
He was going off to Toronto for a lark
But he drove his car into a cement post.
Billy Mykes who always wore torn T-shirts
Also died and so did many others.

19. Sewage Pipe

I remember there were four of us, three
Other guys and me, standing around,
And I didn't know the names of any of them.
There was a huge cement sewage pipe
Coming from the Mountain and down to the shore.
One of the guys started to crawl up
But after a while he couldn't get a purchase.
All of a sudden the water came crashing down.

The guy who was crawling up didn't make it.
He was gone like a flash. And we never
Saw him again. The three of us were stunned.
We just stood silent for hours.
I don't think any of us knew who he was.
If he had parents they never saw him again.

20. Painted Ladies

Franky Forgy was my friend in Grade 10.
He brought a snake to school in a bag.
He put it on the window but Mr. Baxendale
Started screaming because the bag was moving.
What's in that bag? I'll have you out, he said.
I liked Franky because he liked everything
About nature: trees, crickets, and snakes.
He could stare at a leaf for thirty minutes.

Franky was very interested in butterflies.
Soon he was catching Buckeyes and
Acadian Hairstreaks, Painted Ladies,
Northern Pearly-Eyes and all that jazz.
He found a rare Pipevine Swallowtail:
A big find for the Burlington Study Circle.

21. The Eleventh Wave

I'm twelve years old and I'm sitting
On a log on the shore of Lake Erie.
I'm paying attention to the waves.
There is nobody around except for them.
A very small wave comes in and so
A slightly larger wave and then another.
Soon we arrive at the eleventh.
The next wave starts all over again.

The wind is blowing as are the waves
Coming from the smallest to the eleventh
And then back to the smallest again.
Something tells me to turn around.
There's a woman standing on the little cliff:
The wind's blowing her dress between her legs.

22. Mr. Baker

In W. H. Ballard Elementary we boys
Had to spend two hours every week
Sawing boards in half all day long.
It was terribly boring, that's for sure.
We also had to do other things.
We had to make swans out of plastic.
We had to drill holes through thick metal.
Mr. Baker was nice, but very dull.

One day, I was thinking to myself,
And I decided the next time I had
To saw a board I would commit suicide.
I straddled the board and started to cut.
I was planning to cut myself in half.
But Mr. Baker caught me just in time.

2

23. Stars Explode

Now I'm getting old and in a fog
The universe is becoming more peaceable.
Stars explode and worlds collide it's true,
An earthquake or tsunami will ruin your day.
When hunger strikes animals won't hesitate
To slaughter anything that looks like food.
Hungry people will slaughter for revenge.
What's there to say about ignorant armies?

Even as a baby boy in my buggy
I was subject to anxiety attacks
And wanted my parents to push me faster.
And as a kid in my crib I sought to amuse
But it's not like that now I'm getting old.
It makes no difference if things go fast or slow.

24. Mother

I don't know a thing about the dead.
Maybe they are still alive—who knows?
Mother has been dead for twenty years
But maybe she is in some other world.
Now and then I seem to feel her presence
But she never lets me know what's going on.
If there is another happier world
It seems she doesn't want to let me know.

You'll find out soon I can hear her say
But that might only be my sad desire.
Perhaps she's completely forgotten me
And the pain I caused her way back when.
We miss you, Mother. It's sad to see Father
Struggling along without your loveliness.

25. Weekend Hideaway

After anything happens everything becomes
Fictitious, even the notion of the entire
Universe as a Hansel and Gretel cottage
In the bull's-eye of an ancient forest.
Why are the trees and my knees shaking?
What do the hooting howling owls represent?
If the cottage is cosmic, what's the moon?
Every logical system started small.

Members of an obscure society
Of elderly Japanese philosophers
And thousands of tiny Hansels and Gretels
So tiny you could almost step on them
Walk sadly through the dark and rainy forest.
But by Monday they'll be flying back-to-back.

26. Reading One Book Twice

I regret that when I was a little lad
I didn't read more deeply, with more thought,
And with a dictionary at my side,
So that I'd be less tempted to postulate
The momentousness of formidable words.
But when we're ten years old we're in a rush,
Aiming at reading sixty pages per hour,
And reading one book twice was not an option.

Now I'm old the days go faster than death,
Yet I read more slowly than a Buddhist prayer.
It's as if I had all eternity to enjoy.
And now I look up unfamiliar words,
Savour them deeply, slowly, with more thought,
But when they return I've forgotten them.

27. Jailbird

What does it look like now? Have you forgotten
That years ago you spent a year in the can?
You didn't tell a soul but I happen to know
It was the happiest year of your life.
You took your sheets and blankets when you got out
And hitchhiked home on a warm spring day.
People wondered why you were all wrapped up.
The street you lived on seemed transformed.

I'll never have to share that moon again.
I'll never have to read that same book
Over and over until I know every word.
The guy in the diner on my street
Wonders why I'm all wrapped up in blankets.
He asks if I've overdosed on Vitamin Zed.

28. Strange Experiences

Psychoanalyzing generalissimos,
Fuehrers, commanders-in-chief, that sort of thing—
It's a tricky business best done at a distance,
Alone, in the middle of the night.
These guys see evil everywhere they look
Because they never see it in themselves.
You could be disappeared or suicided
For smiling unfitly, or a look in your eye.

But even powerless poets are the same.
The evil in our hearts is not so great
As the evil in the hearts of other poets.
We have little imagination for the suffering
But we have lots of imagination for describing.
Every day there are tons of strange experiences.

29. Mandrake

You always presumed that it would take forever
And you'd have time to do all you want.
Had you the sense you'd be sixty so soon
There are certainties you'd have handled better,
Situations you'd have secured more seriously.
You allowed yourself to suffer deeper sighs
And savour pangs of pain as gentle as rhyme.
A yesteryear can appear without a tear.

But we always knew that you'd turn sixty
And we suspected that you expected it too.
Your desires, Mandrake, have magically vanished,
But you could materialize them in a pinch.
Six-oh's nothing, wait till you're one-six-oh.
Then you'll know what Wisdom's all about.

30. Flashes in the Night

I dreamt a dream of being a firefly
Smiling lazily in the summer night:
Sending messages to all the other flashers
Like something out of *Hannah and Her Sisters.*
And now when I'm sitting silently
Watching my little mind disrobe itself
I feel I'm fluttering naked high in the sky
Free from the agony of gravity.

When our lifelight flashes in the night
We know its span won't be very long.
We live for our brief hour then we die
But when we die we become alive again
And what was once a simple blinking bug
Will conceivably become a dragonfly.

31. Poetic Nastiness

Whoever wins the Boy Scouts animal romp
Will be my friend for all eternity.
I'd like to put a thirty-three-cent stamp
On the forehead of every clown in town.
Normally everyone thinks I'm charming
But my poetics demand nastiness.
What's more important, me or poetry?
Life or death? War or peace? Who can say?

The opposites are not so opposite.
Male or female means practically nothing.
Ask God or Satan if you don't believe me.
Night and day are equally humdrum.
And when you fall asleep tonight remember
You must not tell a lie till you're awake.

32. Heaven

A lovely day in April but I'd prefer
My task of scanning all these photographic
Images of my darling daughter.
Sometimes I'll be walking down the street
Or sitting on the train reading the paper
And I'll hear her lovely voice say Hey Dad!
And I'll say Hi Babe but she'll be gone.
Heaven has no time for earthly beings.

The photos keep reminding me how much
I loved her face, especially her nose.
I called her a liar, someone said.
But I have no memory of that.
We all tell a lie from time to time.
I'm not perfect and nor was she.

33. Sentimentalistics

I wandered through the Forget of Veilfulness
Where salmon on Dexedrine practise their scales
And waterfalls embarrass Viagra patients.
Befuddled assassins, dressed in thongs and sarongs,
Leap from the windows of skeletal skyscrapers
And leave behind this self-same note for the world:
"Once you've learned to perform a difficult skill
You can learn to do it fast and make big dough."

No one will give themselves the time of day.
People who used to swear by their watches
Have smart implants directing them to avoid
Certain views and viewpoints, should they choose
To tinker with the very direction of time
Or to capture those who shoot or practise rhyme.

34. Thunder and Lightning

Christ says let the dead bury the dead
But that to this man sounds a little cruel.
Is Jesus being snide or is it slapstick?
The temperature is millimetring
Its way up and down, clouds taking over,
Getting ready for another downpour.
The lawn-mower fellow's moving really fast.
Thunder and lightning? That would be a blast.

I can't write this garbage anymore.
I have to do something about my life.
But what's to do? Nothing, nothing, nothing.
Maybe this was just a poor translation.
Maybe Christ was saying let the grief-stricken
Continue to be as grief-stricken as they want.

35. More Like Mom Than Pop

I'm not allowed to visit Father till Wednesday:
Not that he's laid up in the hospital
Or behind bars contemplating his crimes
But he's so old it takes him several days
To straighten out his digs for company.
Everyone can relate to that I guess.
He's embarrassed if his place doesn't sparkle,
Not that even at its best it does.

When Mother was alive the place was spotless
And she never seemed to do any cleaning
And never dreamt of having a cleaning lady.
Just the fact that my mother was in her house
Made everything as clean as rhubarb pie.
As for me I'm more like Mom than Pop.

36. Vanished Sights

Why, you funny little darling, I don't know
Who I'm talking about, probably myself.
I wouldn't talk like that about another,
Not even myself and even then not often.
The hours I spent bashing myself on my head
With an empty bottle of Canadian Club
Have dwindled to nothing in the past few years.
I seem to have discovered peace at last.

Shakespeare can grieve at many vanished sights
And drown tears at grievances long foregone
But friends have found new friends and so have I
And may the old live peaceful as the young.
I don't know what it is about peacefulness
But it has embraced me and embraced my friends.

37. I Think to Myself

My head is on the other side of the room,
While I sit here with a book in my hand.
What Remains by Christa Wolf, it's good!
All of a sudden I can't read a word of it!
Where my head was there's only a cloud!
What the heck? What gives? (I think to myself.)
I look around and all of a sudden I see it
Sitting on a mat on the floor by the door.

Thank God I found it. I couldn't live without it.
That'd be even worse than losing my wallet.
I didn't even have to go and get it.
As soon as I found it, it came back to me.
It took its time floating back and re-
Positioning itself perfectly on my neck.

38. Asthmatic Problems

Praise the Lord! I haven't had asthmatic
Problems since I declared the past an illusion.
I think I'll never have another attack.
But something worse will probably come my way,
Like having my penis bit off by an ostrich,
Or being dunked in acid till I have no face.
Have you ever heard of Happytimes' Blessings?
They insist Mother's been better since she died.

We'll be here at midnight visualizing
Death, or trying to. Who knows what's true,
Mother was an admirer of Paul Robeson,
And she was hoping to see him when she died.
At least we've finally come to the conclusion
That time does not exist on Planet Earth.

39. Behind Bars

Now I'm getting older I realize
I've been all along behind bars.
When I was a kid I could ride
Far out into the Niagara Escarpment
But I always had to be back for dinner.
When I was all grown up I could hop
A plane and go anywhere in the world
But anywhere is just the same as here.

I've been appointed as a special delegate
To the International Goodwill Society
But I'll perform my functions here at home
For everywhere I turn I'm behind bars.
Things are probably never going to change
Until my spirit flies off and I'll be free.

40. Sad Sack

Eddie Bracken bought some phonograph needles
From Betty Hutton, and asked her out for a date:
A triple feature at the Regent tonight.
Betty's promised to go to dance with soldiers
Who were going away to fight the Germans.
You'd think they'd throw a party for those,
The ones who stay behind. They also serve,
Those who sit and wait or whatever they do.

Eddie doesn't see Betty as much as he used to.
Betty says come, it's only fifty cents.
But Eddie wouldn't feel right without being
In uniform. He's a sad sack, he's turning to go.
Betty says, hey wait you forgot your needles.
No matter for Eddie. He has no phonograph.

41. Cinematic Babies

Not knowing when my plane will take off,
Not even knowing where's my destination
(I have reason to suspect it's Australia),
Am I the same person I used to be?
Betty Hutton gives birth to six baby boys
In retaliation for the Dionne Quintuplets.
But we love Americans, they're much like us.
My suitcases are full of Australian currency.

What kind of airport is this, I'm wondering.
I took off all my clothes and nobody noticed.
It's so dark, people can't see their money.
We've been waiting here it seems for years,
And if it's not Australia where we're going
Then where the heck it is I'd like to know.

42. Olga's Big Red Bag

A young French woman of Russian descent,
It seemed she wanted to blow herself up.
It was Olga, I'm sure of it. She gave
The audience five minutes to get out.
She said if there was one Israeli who would
Die with her for peace, and not for war,
She'd be happy. Everyone left but her.
She had a big red bag on her shoulder.

She was all alone in the cinema.
The marksman arrived and he shot her dead.
The big red bag contained only books.
It was a fine clear day that day they say.
You could see a thousand miles away.
But nowhere near as far as Olga had gone.

(After Jean-Luc Godard's Notre musique*)*

43. Sadness Forever

Interesting phenomenon when a man
Loves a woman. Where are all these people
Coming from? Spinning balls of slaughter
Full of holes wherein the dead are placed.
It's almost ten years since you died,
Lighthearted, simply because never again
Would you have to suck and gasp for air.
All this oxygen but none for you.

Sometimes people are put in holes alive
In hopes of gaining information from them,
Information they don't want to give
Or information they simply don't have.
At times like that all you can do is pray,
Even if you've never prayed before.

44. Seven Days a Week

Seven days a week I slaved for you
And loved you though you didn't love me much.
Crazy for you sweetie and it didn't bother me
Taking forever for you to love me back.
Then one day I found that you were putting
Strychnine in the baby's pablum. And ground
Glass in the other's scrambled eggs.
That bothered me but I understood.

The babies you remember were adopted.
You'd always been allergic to sexual pleasure.
But were you ever angry when you found me
Scratching myself while watching late-night TV.
So it was an almost perfect marriage
Until your mom and dad insisted I leave.

45. Perfect and Sad

Today Toronto looks perfect and sad
As I walk through the Annex on the way
To meet Jennifer at the pub for a pint.
And I know that if I just continue to walk,
Anywhere in the world I went today
Would look perfectly wretched and sad.
Do not under any circumstances
Put your hand in your pocket abruptly.

With modern science and new-age nutrition
The average age of poets is always increasing.
I learned this today for what it's worth.
You've noticed that before nineteen hundred
Wars were fought by men and after by boys.
At any rate, I like to think that's true.

3

46. Lost Sonnets

Now and then a tiny tear, that's all,
For some sadness from a year ago.
Out of my great sorrow I make little!
People don't know what a nice guy I am
Because I'm prone to be misunderstood.
I wish I could get Vivien back in my life
But then I realize I'm better without her.
A year is very long but then gets short.

If you asked me to tell what the year is
I'd have to stop and see if I could remember.
Anything I've done so far this year?
It's very difficult. Only two things
Come to mind: the death of my daughter
And some sonnets I lost (which I thought were good).

47. Pomegranates

My eyes are like a truck full of pomegranates
Or like a pair of rowboats on the pond,
Sweeter than grapes on a vine or pears on a tree.
How would I live without them I'd like to know,
Or better still I wouldn't want to know.
My thumb-like eyes encompass multitudes.
Friends who have passed away I cannot see
But there are others glad to solace me.

On the street my eyes see many eyes
And occasionally a pair will latch on to mine.
My eyes will sometimes see something I saw
Yesterday and then again today.
I'll see you tomorrow as we like to say
But I don't think our eyes really work that way.

48. Getting Nicer Every Day

Things I used to know are no longer known,
At least not by me or my numerous friends.
I used to know but now I do not know.
Things I never knew before going back
To when I was a baby boy in a bonnet
I've come just recently to know. How odd!
I'd say my friends are in the same position
But who knows what's going on in their minds.

I'm every bit as nice as my nicest friends
But they sometimes get tired of being nice,
While I keep getting nicer every day.
Many long years ago I was never nice
But now there's no one I know nicer than me.
Yet most things—I don't know them anymore.

49. Don't Be Alarmed

I said goodbye to everyone today.
I don't know why, I don't know why I did.
Goodbye even to people I didn't know.
Goodbye to people I hadn't seen in years.
Younger people who find themselves in love,
Or those who feel their love is not returned,
People who are probably dead by now,
People who seem to be looking down from the sky.

And then all of a sudden I realized
I was saying goodbye to all these people.
Honestly, I had no idea why.
It was just that I seemed to want to say it:
Goodbye goodbye goodbye goodbye goodbye.
Don't be alarmed, I'm not about to die.

50. Little Kings

Out of the ambient semi-silence comes
Without the slightest warning a cry of joy
And perfect erotic pleasure and fulfillment.
It was always the Frenchman in the white cap
Who for months was the only one to visit.
But now he's gone and now there is another
And this one's quiet at any time of night,
Or even day unless he's working shifts.

But he makes her laugh. She laughs a lot.
I'd do the same if I were in his shoes.
Don't you love to see your neighbours happy?
Of course you do. Don't we all? Especially
If they're happy just the way they are,
For shouldn't we all be happy as little kings?

51. Valentine Card

Al Capone told it as it was,
Even when he was lying through his teeth.
He was smarter than most intellects around.
No one pushed him into thinking big—
It just came naturally. Racial memory.
Of the poets, he resembled Dylan Thomas.
Of eatables, he looked like a lightly fried
Egg with two unbroken yolks gleaming.

A Renaissance angel with Vishnu components.
He wasn't called Scarface for nothing.
He got those cuts when he was rude to a babe
And her brother pulled a knife and fixed him good.
Hard to dislike a mobster who wasn't a monster
And who ordered the best in funeral wreaths.

52. Eleventh Hour

As long as patches of snow are still around
I love those brilliant days of cold spring.
But once the snow has gone no matter how
Brilliant the day I want it to be warm out.
I know this lacks importance, dearest reader,
Except insofar as it's the sort of thing
Friends may say on days of frozen spring,
When they are walking hand in hand through life.

A patch of snow is shimmering in the sun.
It's hard to imagine this kind of friendship
When we're together more often than we're not.
Everything's okay in my own little life.
All I have to do is smile sincerely
In my eleventh hour and ninth disappointment.

53. Ninth Disappointment

Only we have eyes for the person
Who can do the most for us right away.
Fulfill all our superficial desires
And we'll be phoning forty times a day.
It's hard to live in a world like this
When we can recall something much better.
I like to think that when I'm about to die—
But I have never cared for rushing things.

Kindly spirits will help me find my way
And if they decide that I am not worth it,
Then I'll jump in the dirtiest river in town
And die, but not before I give all my friends
My money, and all my books, and other things.
In our ninth disappointment and eleventh hour.

54. Prohibition

Each word is a leaf on a tree, or
Maybe a valley, a hill, or a river.
All three combined would be popular.
Or a portrait of that gardener at Arles.
Oh to be flecked in soot instead of a
Character in *Metamorphoses*
Or some poor suitor of Penelope
Toothless and bearing boring gifts.

During Prohibition a quart of Canadian
Gin fetched twelve bucks in Chicago.
These verses are designed to appeal:
A true poem only deals in facts
And stems from that refusal to fall apart
(About which nothing can be spoken).

55. Nelson, B.C.

I was way up on a mountain in Nelson
With a bottle of hootch in my pocket
And trying to figure how to get home.
The moon was up higher than an orange
And down below was the roof of a car.
I jumped down on the roof but when I
Landed I must have made a groan.
I fell off the car. I spurted blood.

I turned around, and saw the mom and dad:
Their eyes were popping and the kids' eyes too.
They were shivering as if they saw a ghost.
Their car was lower than I was higher.
I'd broken their antenna on the way down—
Still have the antenna, blood and scars.

56. Parking Ticket

Joys of convalescence: this morning I awoke,
Then made my bed, and collapsed upon it.
First day home from the hospital and I'm
Weak as a teardrop that fell from my nose.
Dreamt that you had something removed, not I.
My time in the hospital? I had intense
Pains in my left elbow and right shoulder.
I shall be here for a while for sure.

I told the doctor it felt as if someone
Had been behind me hammering me on the shoulder.
"No one was standing behind you," he stammered.
When I started writing this poem the sun
Was shining through my bedroom window and now
It's the stars, and now and then the moon.

57. Margaret Laurence

Through his telescope he looks out of the
Window and watches the widowers far and wide.
He seems to be examining their techniques.
What they take and what they leave behind
Will cut down on his learning curve.
When he finds himself completely homeless
He'll know there's nothing he can do about it.
But he looks as if he's about to explode.

He was in a pub, or was it a tub?
At any rate, it wasn't that long ago.
It must have been a lovely situation
Or he wouldn't have remembered all this time.
Yes, he definitely remembered being haunted
By the women in Margaret Laurence's novels.

58. Foolish Blood

In a moment outside time your heart's
Bursting and I'm catching spurting blood
In a golden bowl, or is it just yellow?
We do that a lot, a knife in each eye.
We have arrived, a point in history.
You and I, and maybe others as well.
How can we return to such a mess.
I'm telling it to myself. But I'm a fool.

We exist as blameless as a fact,
I don't mind telling you, it's so true.
Everybody goes to heaven, my friend,
Except for Adolf Hitler— Howdy, Adolf!
These lines will make life more interesting
For all my small-time smudge-pot bohemians.

59. Awareness Now

The slap-happy community of my dreams
Loves to hand out highly publicized
Medals to heroes who made a difference.
Especially the ones who did it for love,
Rather than the lesser sorts of things.
Ah, your cartoon eyes. I could never
Remember which of them was blind.
I'm always somewhere writing juicy poetry.

You used to say I shouldn't be married.
I'm too much of a loner you would say.
In eternal recurrence all the souls
Get to play all the timeless roles.
Sometime new consciousness will invade
Life systems as you and me, my dear.

60. Phoning Rebecca

Rebecca says it's okay to ask for her.
It's a code. These women love their codes.
They're wildly interested in each other.
And so they should be. They are all so different,
Unlike men who are pretty well the same.
I wonder what Rebecca thinks about me.
I do look prosperous in my new hat
Made from coconut fibre from a coconut tree.

Plus in my eyes there's a mischievous glint
That says to any woman looking for it
(The glint that is) you see I'm different
From all the other guys and I'd love
Without causing anyone to throw up
To show you exactly in which way.

61. Galileo's Ox

The French say that if you do your nails
On Monday you'll be healthy. But the Greeks
Say if you do your nails on Saturday
You'll be getting richer and more wealthy.
I'm neither French nor am I Greek
So I thought really hard for a week.
I tossed and turned all through the night
Wondering if my bones were wrong or right.

Then one brilliant day I said I know!
Hurray—I'll do my right hand on Monday,
And I'll leave my left hand till Tuesday.
And that was thirty or forty years ago.
By golly I felt as clever as a fox.
Now I'm tough and as rich as Galileo's ox.

62. Darkened Cinema

For hours we were sitting in a darkened
Cinema arguing loudly and bitterly
And all the other seats were occupied
With sheep and cows and horses and pigs and ducks.
On the screen was *Young Man with a Horn*
But no one was paying attention to anything
Except the sharp sarcasms we were exchanging.
Everything was terribly unpleasant.

I was at a point where it was feasible
To take my life and flick it like a butt,
Go far away where no one would ever know me,
I've got all I need, what am I waiting for?
I'll take up mescal under some volcano
Where I can master the doctrine of No Mind.

63. Romantic Transformations

Eternity created God because
Too many people had too little to eat.
God created time because eternity
Was becoming a little bit boring.
The sorrows of not having enough to eat
Transform defeats into awkward virtues.
Expounding theories is an act of desperation.
I'm waiting for your husband to grow up.

I'm finally out of my romantic period.
Dream and reality have become one.
My next period will probably blend
History, music, and the fear of death.
This is the way I really am. If you
Like this poem include me in your will.

64. With a Line by Horace

It's wrong to dismiss artists on moral grounds.
Those with spotless records in that regard
Simply haven't disclosed the total story.
Shall we refuse to read Mallarmé because
His family paid to keep him out of the army
Or because he greeted his papa's death with a joke?
There's a difference between someone who is dying
And someone who is dead. Take Baudelaire.

He was despised and tormented all his life
But at his funeral declared a genius! Unfair!
Of course it's unfair too that Mallarmé
Said he couldn't tell one anglais from another
Any more than he could the rooms in La Trémoille
And nobody would use that to avoid his verse.

65. Paris Traffic Jam

Titian's Venus and Adonis would make
A wonderful cover for a small
Edition of Shakespeare or Akhmatova.
Except that Adonis isn't quite
Beautiful enough. Titian's that is.
Which reminds me of the need for artists
Of all persuasions to become as actors,
Every dabbler his own Olivier.

Call yourself anything you want
But don't call yourself a poet, my friend.
Apollinaire called the Eiffel Tower
Shepherdess and said her herds of bridges
Were bleating this morning. He was a poet.
And I am just a guy who likes to read.

66. Two Strange Things She Did

Once while visiting my studio she grabbed
A bottle of my Scotch and took a big slug—
Just put it to her lips and sucked it down,
And continued to talk as if nothing had happened.
Once while walking through charming Rosedale
She started pawing through some garbage.
It had been left out for collection.
Then she continued walking without a word.

Given the nature of her being, the actions
Were entirely out of character. In both
Cases it was as if she was extremely
Conscious and unconscious of what she was doing.
For sure I didn't detect the slightest smile.
But maybe I could have been mistaken.

67. A Real Job

See all this hair on my face? This is what
Happens to men when they lose the will to shave.
Simple as nuts. When paralysis strikes
We take the opportunity to do nothing.
Sometimes I think if I had a real job
I'd have to go on leave for a number of months
To get over whatever it is that is
Making me want to have a real job.

I think if I had a real job I wouldn't
Want to have a job for very long.
Something would go wrong, at least, for sure.
I'd very much envy those who have real jobs
But I'd also envy those who have never had one.
I don't think I'm cut out to have a job.

68. Park Plaza

After my five-day fast I put on the pants
I hadn't been able to wear for a few years
And met some friends at the Park Plaza.
We ate numerous bowls of salted almonds
And drank dozens of rounds of martinis
And I kept saying I've never been able to drink
So many martinis without getting smashed.
I told everyone I'd have to fast more often.

Then we switched to beer. And then we had
The worst sushi I ever ate. And washed it down
With that stuff you drink with sushi. Sake?
So that was yesterday. Today I'm going on
Another fast and I've given up martinis.
And maybe even beer and sake and Scotch.

69. Reverend Ratzlaff

My name is David McFadden, and I'm the son
Of William McFadden and the late Elizabeth
Jean McFadden. You will know my father.
I attended St. Paul's Church in my childhood.
I'm now enquiring to see if it would be
Possible for myself and future wife,
Merlin Homer, to be married at St. Paul's.
Merlin has been a widow for many years.

We have a valid Ontario marriage licence.
We live in Toronto. Merlin and I have
Often thought it'd be lovely to be married
At St. Paul's, a church with many memories.
We'll look forward to hearing from you and
Hope you'll be able to accommodate our wishes.

70. Metalanguage

It's something that's about something. Such
As metalanguage is language about
Language. In other words it's one
Degree removed. So metaphysics is
A discussion beyond physics. If physics
Is an explanation of reality
Metaphysics takes that analysis
One step further than physics can go.

If something is a meta-analysis
It would be an analysis of the analytic
Process. A plane flew over the Langley airport
And bombed it with eggs from a height
Of three hundred metres. Some of the eggs
Sported parachutes or hung from balloons.

71. Lake Erie

They took me to an island on Lake Erie.
It couldn't be seen from the Canadian shore.
An airport had been built on this island.
There were hardly any runways, the whole
Island was taken up by the airport,
Which had no elevators but many staircases,
And each staircase marked the spot where
A waterspout was shooting up in the sky.

The airport also doubled as a massive
Library containing every book
Ever printed that related to the history
Of Canada and the United States.
An elderly man in a beaver hat was reading.
The airplane races were getting set to take off.

72. Always in Hallways

The twenty-second century will be a time
Of anonymity, a disappearance
Of the cult of personality.
Names will be forgettable as numbered
Plates on our automobiles today.
One vast nation, everyone working
Together, of course, for survival.
A massive unilateral organization.

Old national identities dissolve
In a sea of separation and sewage.
How bad was the House of Borgia?
In so many ways—and always in hallways—
They seemed extremely happy and aware
Of who they were, and what they were doing.

73. Mister Yellow

I had lunch with Merlin at the Midi.
It was a subtle crusty salmon and we loved it.
Then we went to examine some really amazing
Rocks in somebody's front lawn.
Then we went examining books on tables.
Then I remembered I left my hat at the Midi.
The place was locked so I tapped on the window—
But nobody noticed for the longest time.

So I waited and finally the guy came back.
And another fellow came by and opened the door.
Then I was waiting for a streetcar to come along.
My July Metropass was a beautiful yellow.
Then a car drove by in the same shade of yellow.
And a woman came by wearing the same yellow shirt.

INTERVIEW

INTERVIEW WITH DAVID W. McFADDEN

This email interview, conducted by Stuart Ross from January to March 2005, originally appeared in the poetry mag Syd & Shirley.

When and how did poetry first become important to you?

The only poets I liked were Robert Louis Stevenson in childhood and Shakespeare in adolescence. I loved the idea of poetry, but all the other poets failed to hit the mark somehow. Maybe they didn't even know there was a mark to hit, or so it seemed.

My Grade 5 teacher, at W. H. Ballard in the east end of Hamilton, was a bit of an embarrassment when he would sit on his desk with his legs crossed and read us poems he had written about the squirrels in his backyard. And when he read us "The Death of the Hired Man" by Robert Frost, it made me squirm because it lacked authenticity. Frost was way more interested in the poem than in the sad life and death of the poor old guy. And the farmer's wife was far too intelligent and too nice to be on such good terms with her thoughtless jerk of a husband. Frost seemed oblivious to his own poem, except to admire the cadences, which weren't really all that admirable.

We did a real lot of poetry in high school. When a teacher was teaching us "The Lake Isle of Innisfree" by W. B. Yeats, it also seemed to be inauthentic. And when the teacher told us that Yeats' alliterative line "I hear lake water lapping with low sounds by the shore" was "the greatest line in all of English poetry," I knew something was terribly wrong. When years later I stood on the shore of Innisfree, right by the lake isle itself, there were no lake waters lapping whatsoever, and I don't think there ever had been.

In Grade 9, I won a city-wide prize for an essay on post-Stalin politics in the Soviet Union—Beria, Malenkov, and all that. The prize was an all-day, all-expenses-paid tour of Stelco. So that was good. Then about Grade 11, when people were always saying Canada wasn't a real country because it had no poets, I bravely took the plunge, if not the pledge. Also my kid brother (now a musician) was writing really good Hemingwayesque short stories at the time, so that was egging me on.

From Grade 11 till now I've been writing poems every day, or thinking about it a lot on the occasional day I'd miss. To me an artist had to work every day, it had to be his entire life, or he was a fake. Feel that way even more today.

So I was accumulating all these poems, always trying to figure out ways to make them shine, and to write more and more of them, but the school yearbook editor kept rejecting everything I sent in. So I volunteered for the high school paper, a weekly, and I did all the typesetting and editing. And to retaliate for my snub at the hands of the yearbook editor, I'd delete the basketball scores, and anything else that looked as if it wouldn't be missed, and insert little poems of my own. Nobody complained, nobody commented, nobody seemed to notice.

The poems seem quite amazing and strange in retrospect, though they were very juvenile, of course. Also I was an amateur hypnotist in those days, and I had a girlfriend whom I would hypnotize, and get her reciting remarkable poetry from her deep unconscious, or maybe from her past lives, and then I would type out what she said and put them in the school paper. And that was noticed. In fact, her father was furious.

So then in Grade 13, I sent some tender little lyrics to *Tamarack Review* and they published four of them in the same issue as Anne Wilkinson's "Four Corners of My World." And then I wrote a long adolescent epic called "Danny Quebec" and sent that to *Prism Magazine* and they ran it. My worldview was very working-class, so when cheques from both mags came in on the same day, I figured I'd never have to work a day in my life. Heh heh!

But I was wired much earlier than that, long before I ever dared to write. For instance, I read *Peter Pan* eight times when I was eight years old. And the following year, the first paragraph of *Huckleberry Finn*, where the main character starts critiquing the author, that stunned me, and I felt fabulous portals opening, as a sort of compensation for the gradual loss of childhood's spiritual riches. It used to sadden me beyond sadness that adults couldn't remember their own childhood, and couldn't understand the stuff that was going on in the nasty but fertile little minds of children. I made a serious vow never to forget. I don't think I have forgotten. Everything I've written has a root in childhood.

So you had already published elsewhere (and gotten paid, even!) when you started up Mountain. *Tell me about* Mountain*—I've only ever held one issue in my hands for a few moments at Nelson Ball's bookshop in Paris, Ontario.*

Not much to say, except that the title referred to the Niagara Escarpment, which the locals call the Mountain, with a capital M, Scottish humour. I don't remember much about the magazine, except that it brought in a lot of mail, and it was a totally solo enterprise, worse than juvenile, and I wasted many hours of precious youth working on it for reasons I still don't even wish to understand. But I did learn that there were a lot of Canadian poets, after all. And there I was making friends with all of them. I had to get out of that in a hurry, and I seem to recall in the fourth issue I filled it up with my own poems, with no explanation, then became so Embarrassed with a capital E that I couldn't do another issue, and I didn't.

Seriously, though, I got to know some wonderful people, most of them great geniuses. And I was still living at my mom and dad's house. Milton Acorn popped in one day, took a cigar out of my father's shirt pocket, which my father was wearing at the time, unwrapped it, then put it in his mouth. "Quite the character," said my pa as he offered Milton a light.

That was about as intellectual as the poets would allow themselves to get in public in those days. Expressways and shopping malls were spreading all over North America. Cities were disintegrating.

I realize the embarrassment I feel about *Mountain* relates to the poor quality of attention I was able to give that journal at that time. I was just pushing through, bearing down with more brutality than pleasure, and without the proper sort of care. I had silly ideas about what I was doing, and there was no sense of continuity from issue to issue. At age 21 or whatever, I was still incapable of seeing beyond the little picture. One can't work that way, no matter what one's task may be.

When I decided four issues was enough, I felt very liberated, but it took me forever to begin to understand why.

Were readings a big part of the literary scene back in those days? Do you remember the first reading you gave?

The first one was in a large meeting hall with no furniture, so we had to sit on the floor in a big circle. This was a symbol of something from human culture that had long been pushed back to the level of childhood. To bring it back to adult level was exciting. We were introducing a hint of sanity into the horrors of the post-war economy and a decade of '50s TV. There were about 40 of us in a big circle. No names of anyone there that night rise to the surface. (Wait a minute—Udo Kasemets was there!) It was about 1959 or 1960.

There was a sense of destiny that night, people were tingling all over—maybe it was because there were no guitars or folksingers. We poets abhorred folksingers. We considered them mainstream sissies and loved to make fun of them and leave them off our mailing lists. We deserved everything we got for our cruelty.

People were very nice to me in spite of my lousy poetry, embarrassing metaphors, and extreme youth, and I think I was the only one there without a black-beret/cigarette-holder outfit. The girls had straw baskets and ponytails. I was in my Archie Andrews outfit and was made to feel this was a big deal and I actually did feel very proud and humble to be invited. I was very solemn. This of course was long before the more famous readings in Toronto with Gwen MacEwen, Margaret Atwood, Milton Acorn, Al Purdy. A year at least.

Was there some moment you thought, "Yep, I'm going to be a poet. That's what I'm going to be"? Also, you were a reporter in Hamilton, weren't you? Was that just a way to live while being a poet, or did you consider that writing, as well?

Well, if there was any such moment it would be very early on, in Grade 11 or something like that, as mentioned earlier. But it took me another decade at least before I felt that I could publish my first little book. Before then, I wrote a lot, experimented a lot, but kept almost all of it to myself, and had many frustrations about my work, and had many auto-de-fés. I fed huge reams of my early poems to the flames—a very liberating experience, but still not one bearing much clarity, or much humour either, as I recall.

As for my work at the paper, I was a night proofreader all through the '60s. Sounds odd, but it was a perfect job in many ways. I was a whiz at that and I wish I was still doing it. But then the '60s were over, and I accepted a job as a reporter and stuck at it for five or six years. I sensed that if I didn't accept the reporting job I'd have no job at all, for technical reasons involving the replacement of linotype machines and hot lead with cheap new technologies for putting out a paper with practically no production staff. During those reporting years I was still too raw and politically uneducated to understand what a bad paper, as you can imagine, the *Hamilton Spectator* was in those days. Though it was probably better than it is now.

But I still take pride in certain stories I wrote. And I was famous for working hard. And there were a lot of very fine young reporters working there, getting their start, and some really interesting old-timers.

All of my problems during that period were again due to my inability to understand, to the proper degree, the political nuances at city hall, cop shop, courts, and so on. I'm afraid that in many ways I was an embarrassment to the suits in charge, especially when a furious mayor or police chief would come charging into the managing editor's office to complain about something I'd written.

Can you dig it? I never got fired, but I did get transferred to the Burlington bureau. Also I got sent to the women's department once for a two-week period of punishment, writing about new breakthroughs in lingerie and that sort of thing.

It was a rather boozy time too. Often a high percentage of the newsroom staff would be pissed out of their minds before lunch. I regret that period mostly because of that. I don't think people drink like that anymore. It was scandalous.

I don't know if it's appropriate to mention, but you're my favourite Canadian poet (dividing these things by country lets me have more than one favourite poet). Immersing myself again in your poetry for this interview, I got the same breathless feeling, leaping from poem to poem and book to book, that I got when I first read your work. I might even call it ecstasy.

In the preface to The Art of Darkness *(1984), you write, "Now as never before it's our duty as citizens of the world to subject ourselves to ecstasy, to go beyond and discover the new oceans of ecstasy that lie waiting for the pure pilgrims of love, and to return and talk about it indiscriminately, passionately, like a fundamentalist doorknocker." Do you see your poetry as the reporting back on excursions into ecstasy?*

It's usually perfectly appropriate to offer positive reinforcement wherever you can. It's like love—it makes the world go (a)round, as they say. Unless the person in question is pigheaded and already considers himself the greatest poet of the millennium. So thank you for that. Such a comment couldn't come from a nicer guy, and I'd love to hear more details, not for my own ego but for the sake of the poems.

Reminds me of a few years back—I was in love with a certain woman but she abandoned me because "the world already has enough Samuel Beckett imitators." Your kindness erases that sadness. I'm much more often misunderstood and resented even, seemingly, than appreciated, believe me. Or so it seems from this little mousehole.

No, I no longer see my work in terms of reports from a happier planet, not at all. And when I did see it that way, I was probably under some kind of delusion. In 1984 things were much different. Today I'm more grown-up, more educated, less interested in ecstasy, whatever that used to be, and more interested in devising sets of multiple challenges (of a more or less formal nature) for myself whenever I embark on a new project. It's a bit like shadowboxing. Makes it really interesting. And I almost always win, though it's often a tough long haul. Makes me know for sure I'm alive.

I think this matter of challenging oneself is perhaps even more immediately noticeable in my travel books these days (particularly the *Innocent* series) than in the poems. I usually return home depressed as all get out and under the impression I have nothing to write about. Then when I transcribe the tapes I'm amazed by all the terrific material I didn't know I had. I have buckets of integrity when I write, and never knowingly cheat on myself.

Who are your favourite poets from other countries? Maybe you should invite us all to your next birthday party! We could toss unsigned sonnets into your fedora and you could choose the best one. I'd desperately want to win, but only for nationalistic reasons, of course.

Okay, my favourite poets from other countries. Beyond the U.S., I haven't read enough to make such choices, but what the hell: Ron Padgett (U.S.), Max Jacob (France), Nicanor Parra (Chile), Georg Trakl (Austria), Hans Arp (Germany), Paul Durcan (Ireland), Jaap Blonk (Netherlands).

Wow! Am I ever in good company, eh?

Anyway, I certainly don't get the Samuel Beckett comparison! Aside from the fact that your writing bears no similarity to his, your work is filled with hope. I mean, I love his gloom, but I also love your hope.

We all have our painful awkward insecurities, and for a while I was convinced that yes, she wouldn't have said that unless it were true, I must have been imitating Beckett all along without realizing it. Maybe he'd made this huge impression on me at a subliminal level, and she was the first person to have the courage to tell me I was making an ass of myself by not keeping a respectful distance from the great master. But she might have had Joyce mixed up with Beckett, since I've been a lifelong reader and admirer of Joyce, and I'd never actually read anything of Beckett's until after her comment (although I did see Doug Rodgers' brilliant performance of *Krapp's Last Tape* many years ago).

As for hopefulness, I've never thought of that as being present in my writing, just as it isn't in my life, except to the extent that it's necessary to draw a breath now and then, and have a bite to eat, and try to live within one's means, whatever means happen to be available at any one time. But I go for the light and comic when I can, without thinking of that as hopeful.

In fact, I've always thought of that as part of my essential pessimism, but simply a way of making the composition a bit more bearable both for author and potential reader. Not trying to fool anyone, just as a sort of pleasantry whenever possible, since life has to be lived and why make it worse than it already is.

It doesn't hurt to laugh now and then, even when innocent children are being slaughtered by ignorant armies. There's something decidedly fake, I think, about being perpetually conscious of all the evils of the world. It's almost as if one is forcing oneself into a state of gloom about the state of the world in order to demonstrate one's superior sensitivities. Which is not to say one cannot grieve, and mourn, the monsters and their victims. But let's not make a full-time job out of it. When someone tells a joke, as Thomas Mann says in *Doctor Faustus*, you gotta laugh. You can't beat the guy up for daring to tell a joke at an inappropriate time in history.

Also, there are these articles from time to time in which learned critics discuss McFadden's "dilemma." I've never been able to understand that. Any dilemmas I have are undoubtedly identical with everyone else's dilemmas—remorse, grief, pain, anguish, fear, illness, loss, self-loathing, anxiety, all the dilemmas our flesh and bones and heart and mind can handle, and then some. As a writer I can't see any special dilemmas that I have that others don't—I just write, publish, write, publish, etc., over and over again, until I can't do it anymore, and then shortly after that I sicken, shrivel up, and die. Where's the friggin' dilemma?

But now that you have me thinking of it, maybe you were right and there is hope in my poems. Because, although I'd forgotten, there is in me. In my mind, everything is hopeless. But in my heart there lies slumbering a strange but unerasable sense that somehow the world is going to straighten itself out and a new era of peace and prosperity is about to be born.

You mentioned that these days you like to create formal challenges for yourself with each new project. I see that in Five Star Planet *(2002) more than ever—the huge range of formal structural things going on. But I also went back to the 1977 reissue of* The Saladmaker *(which, for some reason, I remembered as* The Salamander), *and there, in another of your charming prefaces, you talk about how you rewrote the poems, which were originally written a decade earlier: "I would try to figure out what it was I had been trying to say then try to say it in the way I would have said it had I been trying to say it now." You pulled off a similar move just a couple of years ago by rewriting 1982's "The Cow That Swam Lake Ontario" in rhyme. You love to amuse yourself with your own writing! Which is perhaps the magic of your poetry.*

But I wonder if your entire writing career, thus far, and including the fiction, is the result of some compulsion to challenge yourself?

Even though *challenge* seems to be a rather goofy word in this context, yes, for sure, that compulsion exists, always has more or less, and it gives me the steam I need so that I'm continually moving on and not writing the same stuff over and over, if I'm not deceiving myself.

Once upon a time I was something of a musician, a trumpet player, and a piano player, and I got to be technically proficient. But I quit in frustration in my early 20s because I couldn't quite get past the first challenge, that is to enter the first phase of being my own person as a musician. I knocked on that door constantly but it wouldn't open. So finally, without warning, in a very juvenile, irresponsible manner bred of gloom and frustration, I simply didn't show up for a gig one night and I never touched either instrument again. There are things in music you can't be taught, and those were the essential things that would have made all the difference, but they just weren't opening up for me.

As for the poems, at the beginning it was all challenge. It was like being a contestant on *Back Page Challenge* or something like that. I kept bizarre notes on my "progress" as a poet, as if I were trying to get a free game on the pinball machine. And when each series of poems began to lose its initial excitement, and would start sounding dull and stale, why there I'd be knocking on the door again, and the door would open, and I'd be into a new stage, and I'd find myself stepping into a new world that was the same as the old world, but with a more interesting way of demanding to be looked at, or a strangely different atmosphere. Colours and smells would be different, and a fresh new range of stuff would present itself for my inspection.

And as each door would open I'd get into other things besides simply challenges. I'm not sure what these other things were just now, or maybe I just don't have the energy to name them just now, but you will no doubt have the general idea already.

So this kept going on and on, and anyone who may care to do so can see the trail I left behind in the books I wrote. And even today, I still feel like a junior air cadet, as if I had more discoveries and thrills and chills as a poet ahead of me than behind me. Odd, that.

Of course one of these days I'm going to meet my Waterloo and that'll be it. Then I can retire and spend the rest of my life watching TV night and day and taking my dog to visit people on the psychiatric ward.

But you are right, one of the nicest things was to take a poem I found worthy that I had written in a previous phase, and transform it into a phase that was new and fresh to me. Such as with "The Cow That Swam Lake Ontario."

I haven't done that a lot, because I haven't had the sense that there are a lot of poems that would bear that transformation without becoming overly artificial. I have to feel very inspired to try that trick. I have to feel very good about the possibilities, as if I can almost hear the poem begging for a whole new chance in a whole new world that has only recently opened up. And that woman I mentioned earlier, she was always complaining about poets who keep writing the same poem over and over.

I remember, a few years back, spending an excellent afternoon with you in Ottawa, wandering through the War Museum and the National Gallery. You sure know a lot about paintings. And you have a beautiful Alan Dayton portrait of you on the cover of There'll Be Another, *and the inside covers of that book reproduce a painting by Greg Curnoe, with whom you were very close and with whom you collaborated on* Animal Spirits *and* The Great Canadian Sonnet.

It all ties together for me when I read your poems "New York" and "Frank O'Hara" from The Art of Darkness. *Like the New York Poets, you seem to have a real affinity for painters. Do you see a connection between their art and your art? Are there painters that care about poetry?*

These questions bring tears to my eyes. Things are changing, Stu. Or maybe they have changed, period. The Canadian Belle Epoque is over and done with.

But yes, I remember vividly that lovely day we spent together at the War Museum and the National Gallery. Oddly enough it was Remembrance Day 2001. We were both a little low on energy, as I recall, but we certainly made the most of what we had. On that particular day it seemed that all the best work owned by the National Gallery was in storage or out on loan (more likely the former). But some of the stuff on display was worth a glance or two, and maybe even a moment's thought. The more historical stuff was the most interesting, as I recall, but that may have simply been the luck of the draw on that particular day.

For years I couldn't help noticing that whenever I discovered a new poet I admired, he or she, as it would turn out, would be vitally interested in current painting—invariably, though I never did manage to work out a theory of why that should be so. And all the interesting painters were interested in poetry—everyone from Greg Curnoe to Jackson Pollock and so on. It was simply unthinkable not to be; it was second nature to be curious about what everyone was doing. That input was essential as food and drink. There were some painters who weren't interested in poetry, such as the prominent Painters 11 group in Toronto of the '50s. But all the people who were doing intelligent and original work were interested in any other intelligent and original work they could find, and whether it was in the form of painting or poetry or music, it didn't matter. The good stuff set off beautiful little explosions in the mind.

Meanwhile, such fabulous and wildly original painters as John Boyle, now well into his 60s, is still working away in his studio, and his work just keeps getting more and more interesting, but nobody's very interested. In fact, the last batch of paintings he sold, if I have this story right, and it's from the horse's mouth, the guy who bought the paintings didn't even look at them. Not when he bought them, not when they were delivered to his home, and not when he ordered them to be stored permanently in his basement. He only bought them, through an agent, for a tax break. Oh, the ignominy! Even though, according to my understanding, you can't claim a tax break on a painting unless it's hanging in your place of work, not wrapped in plastic behind the furnace.

Boyle still does his best to pay attention to other painters, and even to the poets—but it's difficult for him and very sad. But to his credit, and the credit of many others, such as Robert Fones, they're still painting and their work keeps getting more and more interesting—to those of us who care to pay attention from time to time. And even then it's not easy to visit their studios to check out their latest work, because of the aura of sadness about how our civilization has become so warped and so ignorant over the past decade or two. You just have to keep going, and tease yourself with vain hopes that someday far in the future all this work will mean something to someone once again.

I've already said too much and I have no desire to demoralize anyone, but that's the way I see things.

What makes a good poem? And can the recipe be bottled and sold?

Any formula for making a good poem can only be expressed in terms of tongue-in-cheek comedy, such as E. M. Forster's notion that a poem must create some kind of comparison between humanity and flowers. In real terms it's a field as wide as the human universe, and anything at all, from dead dogs to doorknobs to ploughed fields to pre-emptive strikes, can experience the pleasure of being transformed into brilliant verse at the hand of a good poet.

As for poems becoming commodities, I suppose that can only happen either after a poet is dead, and then only one time out of a thousand, or after a poet has won the Nobel Prize, with much better odds, I suppose—maybe one time out of ten. However, if you can single-handedly start a whole new school of poetry, then your chances are much greater.

Probably a poet has a better chance of being turned into a commodity than any of his poems will have. I mean, look at you, Stu. You're a bit of a commodity, wouldn't you say? You know how to bottle and sell yourself probably better than you know how to bottle and sell your poems, am I right? Personally I don't think I have what it takes either to bottle and sell myself or my poems, so I'm definitely not the right guy to be attempting to answer such interesting questions.

Okay, David, I shouldn't have included the "bottled and sold" part! I think what I was really getting at was whether the qualities that make a good poem could be taught. Probably I should have said just that. But I still found your answer interesting, and I would argue that your poems are so compelling and accessible that they sell themselves. Whether or not the books sell is a whole other story.

But getting back to the first part—and with a little word transposition for clarification—what makes a poem good? Whether it's by you or John Donne or Gil Adamson or Frank O'Hara.

Each line must bring a fresh surprise and possess the dynamics of a good haiku, and the final line must leave the reader cumulatively stunned and short of breath, maybe even transfigured for a minute or two, and maybe changed forever.

Do you think about audience when you write?

I think only of that famous audience of one, myself, when I'm committing the first draft to paper. In subsequent drafts I think more and more of this audience you speak of and less of myself. That way I'm less likely to embarrass myself and the audience. Also, I should add that this mythical audience (in my mind, most of them haven't even been born yet) is always composed of people who are just like me, but they don't know me at all. So that way playing to the audience is a lot like writing for myself, except that I try to get rid of the boring stuff that would only be interesting to my own little self, such as sentimental slop, excessive vanity, and other forms of nastiness, wrong notes, and traces of halitosis and dandruff.

Wow, I have trouble imagining people I don't know reading my poems!

Last question, and a predictable one, I'm afraid: can you tell me about any current or future projects?

I've just finished the "final" draft of *An Innocent in Cuba*, which will be out in June. It's the fourth of the *Innocent* series. It was supposed to be out by now, but I had a serious fall last summer and have been having trouble recovering properly. I'm close to 90 per cent now, but still walking with a cane just as a little bit of insurance.

I wrote a series of 38 sonnets last year, but can't seem to get back to them this year. It just doesn't seem worth it unless I'm enthused, and I haven't been all that enthused lately about the poems. Not sure I even understand them.

Well, 38 Sonnets *sounds like a great title for a book! David, thanks so much for taking the time to answer these questions over the past month. I know you've been a busy guy.*

Thank you, Stu. You're a good guy. It was a thrill to be interviewed by you, and to know that this is going to be in the first issue of a magazine actually named after your parents.

Acknowledgements

I would like to thank Stuart Ross and Merlin Homer, without whose support there would be no books.

David W. McFadden has been publishing poetry since the early 1960s. He is the author of over 30 books of poetry, fiction, and travel writing. *Why Are You So Sad? Selected Poems of David W. McFadden* (Insomniac Press) was shortlisted for the 2008 Griffin Prize for Poetry, and *Be Calm, Honey* (Mansfield Press) was shortlisted for the 2009 Governor General's Award for Poetry (his third such nomination). In 2013, *What's the Score?* (Mansfield Press) won the Griffin Prize for Poetry. David lives in Toronto with his wife, the singer and visual artist Merlin Homer.

OTHER BOOKS FROM MANSFIELD PRESS

Poetry

Leanne Averbach, *Fever*
Tara Azzopardi, *Last Stop, Lonesome Town*
Nelson Ball, *In This Thin Rain*
Nelson Ball, *Some Mornings*
Gary Barwin, *Moon Baboon Canoe*
George Bowering, *Teeth: Poems 2006–2011*
Stephen Brockwell, *Complete Surprising Fragments of Improbable Books*
Stephen Brockwell & Stuart Ross, eds., *Rogue Stimulus: The Stephen Harper Holiday Anthology for a Prorogued Parliament*
Diana Fitzgerald Bryden, *Learning Russian*
Alice Burdick, *Flutter*
Alice Burdick, *Holler*
Jason Camlot, *What The World Said*
Margaret Christakos, *wipe.under.a.love*
Pino Coluccio, *First Comes Love*
Marie-Ève Comtois, *My Planet of Kites*
Dani Couture, *YAW*
Gary Michael Dault, *The Milk of Birds*
Frank Davey, *Poems Suitable to Current Material Conditions*
Pier Giorgio Di Cicco, *The Dark Time of Angels*
Pier Giorgio Di Cicco, *Dead Men of the Fifties*
Pier Giorgio Di Cicco, *The Honeymoon Wilderness*
Pier Giorgio Di Cicco, *Living in Paradise*
Pier Giorgio Di Cicco, *Early Works*
Pier Giorgio Di Cicco, *The Visible World*
Salvatore Difalco, *What Happens at Canals*
Christopher Doda, *Aesthetics Lesson*
Christopher Doda, *Among Ruins*
Glen Downie, *Monkey Soap*
Rishma Dunlop, *The Body of My Garden*
Rishma Dunlop, *Lover Through Departure: New and Selected Poems*
Rishma Dunlop, *Metropolis*
Rishma Dunlop & Priscila Uppal, eds., *Red Silk: An Anthology of South Asian Women Poets*
Ollivier Dyens, *The Profane Earth*
Laura Farina, *Some Talk of Being Human*
Jaime Forsythe, *Sympathy Loophole*
Carole Glasser Langille, *Late in a Slow Time*
Eva HD, *Rotten Perfect Mouth*
Suzanne Hancock, *Another Name for Bridge*
Jason Heroux, *Emergency Hallelujah*
Jason Heroux, *Memoirs of an Alias*
Jason Heroux, *Natural Capital*
John B. Lee, *In the Terrible Weather of Guns*
Jeanette Lynes, *The Aging Cheerleader's Alphabet*
David W. McFadden, *Be Calm, Honey*
David W. McFadden, *Shouting Your Name Down the Well: Tankas and Haiku*
David W. McFadden, *What's the Score?*
Kathryn Mockler, *The Purpose Pitch*
Leigh Nash, *Goodbye, Ukulele*
Lillian Necakov, *The Bone Broker*
Lillian Necakov, *Hooligans*
Peter Norman, *At the Gates of the Theme Park*
Peter Norman, *Water Damage*
Natasha Nuhanovic, *Stray Dog Embassy*
Catherine Owen & Joe Rosenblatt, with Karen Moe, *Dog*
Corrado Paina, *The Alphabet of the Traveler*
Corrado Paina, *Cinematic Taxi*
Corrado Paina, *The Dowry of Education*
Corrado Paina, *Hoarse Legend*
Corrado Paina, *Souls in Plain Clothes*
Nick Papaxanthos, *Love Me Tender*
Stuart Ross et al., *Our Days in Vaudeville*
Matt Santateresa, *A Beggar's Loom*
Matt Santateresa, *Icarus Redux*
Ann Shin, *The Last Thing Standing*
Jim Smith, *Back Off, Assassin! New and Selected Poems*
Jim Smith, *Happy Birthday, Nicanor Parra*
Robert Earl Stewart, *Campfire Radio Rhapsody*
Robert Earl Stewart, *Something Burned on the Southern Border*
Carey Toane, *The Crystal Palace*
Aaron Tucker, *Punchlines*
Priscila Uppal, *Sabotage*
Priscila Uppal, *Summer Sport: Poems*
Priscila Uppal, *Winter Sport: Poems*
Steve Venright, *Floors of Enduring Beauty*
Brian Wickers, *Stations of the Lost*

Fiction

Marianne Apostolides, *The Lucky Child*
Sarah Dearing, *The Art of Sufficient Conclusions*
Denis De Klerck, ed., *Particle & Wave: A Mansfield Omnibus of Electro-Magnetic Fiction*
Salvatore Difalco, *Mean Season*
Paula Eisenstein, *Flip Turn*
Sara Heinonen, *Dear Leaves, I Miss You All*
Christine Miscione, *Carafola*
Marko Sijan, *Mongrel*
Tom Walmsley, *Dog Eat Rat*
Corinne Wasilewski, *Live from the Underground*

Non-Fiction

George Bowering, *How I Wrote Certain of My Books*
Denis De Klerck & Corrado Paina, eds., *College Street–Little Italy: Toronto's Renaissance Strip*
Pier Giorgio Di Cicco, *Municipal Mind: Manifestos for the Creative City*
Amy Lavender Harris, *Imagining Toronto*
David W. McFadden, *Mother Died Last Summer*
Deborah Verginella, ed., *Bon Appetito Toronto!*

For a complete list of Mansfield Press titles, please visit mansfieldpress.net